# FOR YOUR GARDEN

ERECTED BY
CARLYLE CONCRETE Co Ltd
183 ST VINCENT ST
GLASGOW

...ONALLY
...CAMPAIGN
...ROVIDE
...SHELTERS
...TE HOUSES

...ERIALS AVAILABLE
...TS

...E SHELTER TO BE
...OF YOUR FAMILIES

...FORMWORK DETAILS
...US

GARDEN
A.R.P. SHELTERS
GIVING
MAXIMUM PROTECTION
AT MINIMUM COST

...E APPROVAL
...OVERNMENT

...K BLAST
...O DEBRIS
...BUILDING

...HELTER

...CCUPANTS

...CESSIBLE
...TROUBLE

...Y —

...IN
...E

# Scotland in

**Cover:** [main] The Commando War Memorial at Spean Bridge in the Highlands; [inset] two evacuees leaving Glasgow at the start of the war.
**Endpapers:** Inspecting a new concrete air-raid shelter in Glasgow, 1941.
**Contents page:** Bombed-out and homeless in Clydebank, 1941.

First published in 1997 by Wayland Publishers Ltd, 61 Western Road, Hove, East Sussex BN3 1JD, England

**British Library Cataloguing in Publication Data**
Dargie, Richard
    Scotland in World War II. – (Scottish History)
    1. World War, 1939–1945 – Scotland – Juvenile literature
    2. Scotland – History – 20th century – Juvenile literature
    I. Title
    941.1'084

ISBN 0 7502 1874 6

**Editor:** Carron Brown
**Consultant:** Iain Hall, PGCE Primary Course Co-ordinator, Faculty of Education, University of Paisley
**Designer:** Joyce Chester

Typeset by Joyce Chester
Printed and bound in Italy by G. Canale C.S.p.A., Turin

**Picture Acknowledgements**
The publishers gratefully acknowledge the permission of the following to use their pictures in this book: Aberdeen Journals Ltd 10, 19, 21, 30, 35, 38 (both), 40; Caledonian Newspapers Ltd *cover* (inset), *endpapers*, *contents page*, 13 (both), 14, 15, 17, 18, 22 (top), 23 (top), 31, 32 (right); D. C. Thomson & Co. Ltd 24, 41 (bottom); Hulton Getty 7; Imperial War Museum, London 20 (top), 22 (bottom), 25, 28, 29, 32, 33, 34 (bottom), 41 (top); Popperfoto 11, 20 (bottom); The Scottish Highland Photo Library *cover* (main), 39 (both); Topham Picturepoint 16; Wayland Picture Library 8, 23 (bottom).

A special thank you to the *Press and Journal*, Aberdeen and Caledonian Newspapers Ltd, Glasgow for the time taken to research photographs for this book. A special thank you also to D. C. Thomson & Co. Ltd for allowing us to use *Oor Wullie* sketches.

Artwork supplied by: Peter Bull Art 9, 12; Catherine Parsons chapter logo artwork and cover artwork; Mark Peppé 4–5, 26–27, 36–37; Sallie Alane Reason 45.

# World War II

## Contents

# Blitz on the Clyde

There was a bright, full 'bombers moon' which lit up the dark, March sky. The leading German pilot peered through the glass of his cockpit. All of western Scotland lay beneath him. The towns were blacked out, but the moonlight was shining on the River Clyde, lighting up the land below like a map. The pilot could see his target. It was nine-thirty in the evening.

Around 8,000 ft (2,438 m) below, the people of Clydeside heard the wailing sirens that warned them that Nazi bombs were on the way. Meals were left half-eaten on kitchen tables, radios crackled in empty rooms, as families hurried to the shelters 'in the backies'. The blitz had come to Scotland.

The first bombs were fire sticks that helped mark out a path for the German bombers behind them to follow. Singer's huge factory at Clydebank was one of the first to be hit. John Brown's shipyard and the weapons factory at Dalmuir were soon burning fiercely. In the streets of Clydebank, fire crews and police struggled throughout the night to put out the flames.

At dawn, the damage became clear. Around 1,200 Clydesiders were dead, and another 2,000 were injured. In Clydebank, only a handful of houses were undamaged. About 35,000 people were homeless. Great fires raged from the factories and warehouses where much of Scotland's war material was made and stored.

The first task was to find any survivors amongst the rubble and to bury the dead. Key services, such as water, that had been cut off in the bombing had to be repaired. Blitzed survivors made their way to makeshift rest centres where there was tea, food and a chance to sleep. Then they had to evacuate their homes, before darkness fell and the bombers returned. It was March 1941 and Scotland was at war.

Tenements reduced to burning rubble in Clydebank, 1941.

# The Coming of War

In 1918, World War I in Europe ended. Around 10 million Europeans had died. Most people never wanted war again. Even in Germany, the country that had lost World War I, most people wanted peace. But one man, a soldier in the German army, wanted revenge. His name was Adolf Hitler.

Hitler was angry that Germany had lost World War I and had then been punished by the victorious Allies of France, Great Britain and the USA. Germany had lost some of its land after the war. This land had been given to Germany's more peaceful neighbours. Many Germans now found themselves living in foreign countries. Hitler wanted a war to recapture these lost territories.

Hitler believed that the Germans were the 'Master Race'. He believed that they should rule over the other peoples of Europe. He wanted a war so that he could conquer the other European nations.

Above: Adolf Hitler, the Führer or leader of Germany from 1933–45.

Right: Map of Nazi-occupied land 1939–41.

In the 1930s, millions of Germans were unemployed and hungry. They wanted a strong leader who would make their country great again. In 1933, Hitler became the leader, or Führer, of Germany. He soon began to build up Germany's armed forces in preparation for war.

In March 1938, Hitler sent his troops to invade Austria, which then became part of Germany. He began to threaten Czechoslovakia and Poland. The French and British tried to prevent another war.

The British Prime Minister, Neville Chamberlain, even flew three times to Germany in the autumn of 1938 to try and stop war breaking out.

On 1 September 1939, Hitler attacked Poland. Britain and France had promised to help Poland if war started. On 3 September, Chamberlain spoke sadly to the peoples of the British Empire on the BBC radio to tell them that war with Germany had begun. This news was to change the life of every single person living in the British Empire.

# Joining Up

Long before September 1939, the British government had been getting ready for war. In 1938, war had almost broken out when Germany invaded Austria. Over one million men and women had already volunteered to join the armed forces. By the time the war started, they had already completed their basic training. However, many more people were needed to join the Royal Navy, the Royal Air Force (RAF) and the army.

Once war was declared, the government passed a National Service law. All men between eighteen and forty years old had to put their names on a register, then report to a military inspection centre. The menfolk from almost every family in Scotland were soon in uniform again, only twenty years after World War I had ended. One couple from Ayr had seven sons, two son-in-laws, two grandchildren and twelve nephews in the armed services.

Young Gordon Highlanders queuing for their rations at a training camp, in 1939.

Royal Scots having a break during a training exercise in England, 1940.

Many new recruits soon began to arrive at their barracks. Their training was tough at first. Some regiments were short of uniforms, boots and ammunition. Many new soldiers were issued with old equipment that had been in storage since the last war. Many of the older officers had fought in the last war. They thought the war would be fought like World War I, in trenches. All over Scotland, soldiers were practising how to dig and defend trenches as their fathers had done in 1914. Unfortunately, Hitler was planning a faster, modern style of war using tanks and aircraft.

By late September, 1939, the first battalions were on their way to France. Cheery, confident Scots soldiers waved goodbye to their friends and families at railway stations and ports around the country. Within days, they were in a fascinating new world across the English Channel. For most of these Scots soldiers, it was the first time they had been abroad. Until the serious fighting started, in May 1940, the war was almost a holiday for many young Scots soldiers. The British even called it the Phoney War.

# The Threat from the Air

When the war started, everyone all over Britain was worried about being bombed by the Luftwaffe. Lights on the ground helped German pilots find their way at night to their targets. The government passed blackout laws which meant that no lights were to be shown after sunset. Families had to hang thick curtains over their windows. The police and the Air Raid Precaution (ARP) squads patrolled the streets every evening to make sure no light was showing. One Clydebank woman was fined in court because her cat had brushed against a switch and turned on a light by accident. There were no street lamps, or car lights either. Some people were killed in traffic accidents. Later, trees, kerbs and lampposts were painted white to help drivers see in the blackout.

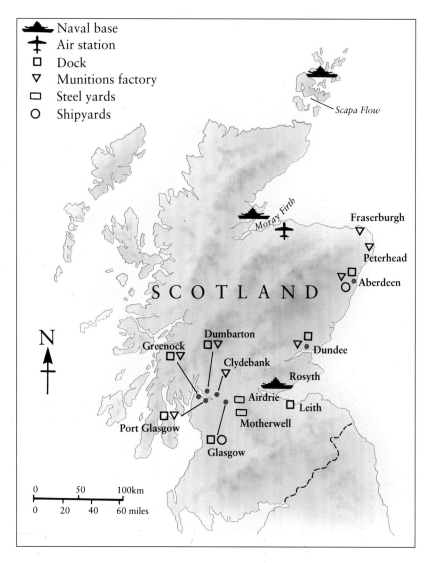

Legend:
- Naval base
- Air station
- □ Dock
- ▽ Munitions factory
- ▭ Steel yards
- ○ Shipyards

Scapa Flow

Moray Firth

Fraserburgh

Peterhead

Aberdeen

SCOTLAND

N

Dumbarton

Greenock

Clydebank

Dundee

Rosyth

Airdrie

Leith

Port Glasgow

Motherwell

Glasgow

0    50    100km
0   20   40   60 miles

This map shows the main Scottish targets that the Luftwaffe wanted to bomb. These places were all very important to the allied war effort.

Public air-raid shelters were built in all the larger Scottish towns. In Edinburgh, shelters were built under Princes Street Gardens. Around 20,000 tenement closes in Glasgow were made into places of safety using steel huts and sandbags.

Air-raid shelters were inspected to make sure they were deep enough.

Tenement doorways and closes were protected with walls of sandbags.

Many families bought shelters for themselves. Anderson shelters came in kit form and cost £7. They were made from corrugated steel and were safe, unless they were hit directly by a bomb. Many Scots families had shelters in their back gardens, but in the high Glasgow tenements, some people preferred to build shelters in their bedrooms.

The government was worried that the Germans would drop poison gas on to towns and cities. Even before the war began, most Scottish families had been equipped with gas masks. Everyone was trained how to put on their gas masks as quickly as possible. Children had to carry them to school every day or risk being punished by their teachers.

Scottish schoolchildren trying out their new gas masks.

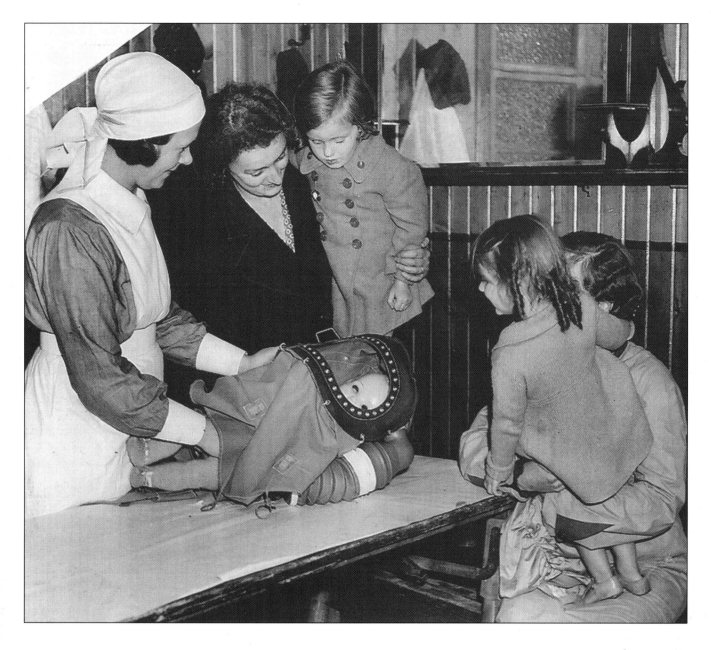

The blackout was unpopular but it worked when there was not a full moon. Most German raiders found it difficult to hit the factories and shipyards which were their main targets. The shelters worked too. People soon got used to running into them for safety when the warning sirens blew. Although some shelters were hit, they saved thousands of injuries from flying glass and shrapnel.

**Gas suits were made for young children who were too small to wear gas masks.**

Many families grew used to their shelters. Some even grew flowers around the entrances. However, gas masks were never popular. Children were scared by them. Fortunately, they were never used as the Germans did not drop their dreaded gas bombs.

# Getting the Children Away

The government knew that Germany planned to bomb British cities that had important targets such as shipyards and factories. They suspected that Glasgow, Edinburgh, Dundee, Clydebank and Rosyth were likely to be bombed. These Scottish towns had important government buildings in them, and factories making supplies that were needed for the war.

There was a great fear of air bombing at the start of the war. Everyone had seen cinema newsreel pictures from the Spanish Civil War in 1936–39.

These newsreels showed how modern bomber planes could destroy a city and kill tens of thousands of people in minutes. The government expected a huge number of deaths and injuries from German air raids.

In a blitz, people could be killed by the blast of a bomb, by fire and fumes, or if their home collapsed on them.

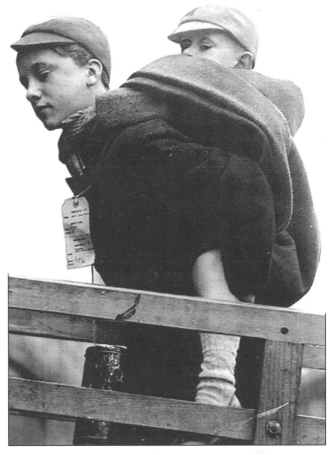

Every evacuee had a name tag, a gas mask and a small supply of rations.

The government decided to move children away from threatened town areas to safer places in the countryside. Their parents would know they were safe in small country towns and farms where the Germans would not bomb. This was called evacuation. Thousands of British children were evacuated. They were taken from their homes and sent away on trains and buses. A name label was pinned on each child. They carried their gas masks and a bag with some spare clothing. Each child was allowed to carry one favourite toy.

Edinburgh schoolchildren and their teachers moving out of the city, in 1939.

Soon the children and their teachers arrived at their new wartime homes. Sometimes, evacuees went to live with relatives, but most children were sent to volunteer families who had agreed to take them in. Most Scottish evacuees went to villages in Aberdeenshire, Ayrshire, Perthshire, the Borders and the Highlands.

Some children settled quickly in their new homes and were glad they were safe from the bombing. They looked on the evacuation as an adventure. Many city children had rarely been in the countryside before. Sadly, many children became homesick and missed their parents. Others did not get on with the new families they were living with and were soon very unhappy.

By 1940, the government had realized that the bombing in Britain was not as bad as everyone had feared. Parents wanted their children back home with them again, rather than living far away with strangers. By 1941, most of the Scottish evacuees were back with their parents again.

Parents took their children to bus and railway stations, not knowing if they were going to see them again.

# Doing Your Bit

World War II was a total war. This means that everyone was involved, not just the men and women in the armed forces. Everyone in Scotland could do something to help the war effort.

Some men, such as coal-miners and policemen, were in special 'reserved' occupations. They were doing important jobs that already helped the country so they were not allowed to join the armed forces. Other men were too old or were not fit enough to fight. However, they could 'do their bit' by joining the Land Defence Volunteer Force or Home Guard. These were part-time soldiers who trained in their spare time and guarded important buildings. Others joined the ARP squads that made sure the blackout was kept by everyone and helped the fire brigade rescue survivors of raids.

Government posters encouraged everyone to help with the war effort.

Children had their part to play too. The BBC asked children to watch out for Nazi spies and to help squash rumours of invasion by Germans. In farming areas, schools closed at harvest time and the children were sent 'to lend a hand on the land'. Most of the men who took in the harvest before the war were fighting abroad in the armed forces.

Home guardsmen protecting a bridge and road junction in Edinburgh, 1941.

Thousands of young Scots joined organizations like the Girl Guides and Boys Brigade. They did a lot of important war work such as helping at relief stations after air raids. They gave first aid and tea to the slightly wounded, then checked that fire buckets had been refilled with water or sand. Others worked in hospitals, helping the cleaners and the kitchen staff. When there was a shortage of materials, they organized collections of waste products to recycle them. Tonnes of silver paper, cotton reels and scrap metal were collected by children so that they could be turned into weapon parts. Many Scottish children won a War Service Badge in this way.

Even the rich and famous had to do their bit. Famous entertainers and film stars of the time often used their talents in the war effort. They gave free performances to soldiers and to factory workers to help keep up everyone's spirits.

**The Boys Brigade in Aberdeen collecting waste paper and metal for recycling,**

# Making Do on the Rations

When war broke out, Britain was short of many important war supplies such as petrol, food and metal for weapons. In 1940, German submarines sunk hundreds of supply ships carrying food from abroad, many of them off the west coast of Scotland at the mouth of the River Clyde.

The government was worried that Britain might be starved into surrender. Food had to be rationed to make sure everyone got a fair share. Every family was given a Ration Book. It was made up of paper tokens. People had to register with their local butcher and grocer. They had to have the right number of tokens to buy rationed foods that were in short supply. These included sugar, butter and meat. Luxury foods such as sweets and fresh fruit were almost impossible to find. Scottish children grew up during the war years never knowing what an orange or banana looked or tasted like.

The Government encouraged everyone not to overeat, and to never leave food on the plate.

A clear plate means A clear conscience

Don't take more than you can eat

A Glasgow family opening a parcel of tinned and dried foods sent from friends in America.

Government clerks had to send out and check ration tokens from every family and shop in Scotland.

Sugar, cheese, butter, margarine, lard, bacon and an egg – one adult's rations for a week.

There was no shortage of the foods that could be grown in Scotland, such as potatoes, turnips and barley. Even in towns, people were encouraged to 'dig for victory' by planting vegetables in their gardens. Councils sometimes ploughed up local parks to plant 'greens'. Fish was never rationed, so many Scottish communities around the coast had a plentiful supply of food from fishing. Even so, nothing could be wasted. All food scraps were kept to be made into a 'hot pot' or fed to the pigs.

Some Scots tried to vary their diet by using unusual foods such as nettle soup or dandelion fritters. Many Scottish children grew up on 'potted heid', meat boiled off the head of a sheep or cow and then set in jelly. Whale meat was tried at one point during the war but it was not popular. To save wheat, a National Loaf was introduced in 1942 which was grey in colour, rather than white. Many people kept rabbits and pigeons as a way of getting extra meat. There were always 'firewood sausages' to eat. These got their name because they were mostly filled with bread and they fried up and burnt very quickly.

# Keeping Your Chin Up!

Every Scottish family suffered during the war. At times, there was a lot of bad news. Allied troops often suffered terrible losses. Everyone had friends and relatives who were killed or captured. Then there was the death and misery caused by German bombing. People on the Home Front in Scotland had to keep up their spirits. They had to believe they were winning the war.

A lot was done to keep people cheery. Winston Churchill, who was Prime Minister from 1940–45, and members of the Royal Family toured Scotland to encourage workers and praise them. Favourite comic characters, such as Oor Wullie and The Broons, were shown

**Oor Wullie and his pals making a fool of the Nazis in *The Sunday Post*.**

doing their bit for the war effort. Captured enemy tanks and planes were put on show in all the main towns. Public parades were held to cheer everyone up. There were wall posters everywhere reminding people that Hitler was going to lose the war. Popular songs, such as 'We'll Meet Again', promised that the war would end some day and life would get back to normal.

The government strictly controlled news about the fighting in the war. Newspapers everywhere, including Scotland, had to be very careful about how they reported the war. They described British victories but said little when Allied troops were defeated. Cinema films, newsreels, novels and magazines told people at home about the bravery of British servicemen.

A famous comedian and singer, Sir Harry Lauder, entertaining workers at a Glasgow shipyard, in 1941.

Photographs in newspapers always showed our troops smiling and in good spirits. German soldiers were always shown as being cruel or stupid. This is called propaganda. People were only allowed to see and hear about the war what the government wanted them to. People disliked the Germans and felt that the British troops would be victorious.

The Germans also broadcast propaganda radio programmes to Scotland from Germany. One Nazi newsreader was called Lord Haw-Haw by the British because of his posh English accent. He tried to depress his listeners. He claimed that the Germans were winning the war easily. After 1942, no one really believed what he said. Most people believed the BBC was more truthful.

# Training in the Highlands

In the summer of 1940, the British army in Europe was defeated and had to retreat from Dunkirk in the north of France back across the English Channel. It was not until 1944 that a large Allied force returned to France. In the years between, the Allies could only make short raids into Nazi-held Europe. The raids were made by soldiers with special skills called Commandos. They landed secretly at night to destroy railway lines, bridges and buildings of importance to the German war effort. These Commandos were trained in Scotland.

The Commandos needed to be tough and able to fight in the hardest climates. They had to know how to live off the land, how to disguise themselves and how to avoid being spotted by the enemy. The western Highlands, a land of rough mountains and moorlands, was the perfect training ground for these men.

The first Commandos were selected from the Scots Guards, the Gordon Highlanders and the Seaforth Highlanders. These men knew the wild Scottish countryside well. They were joined by one of Scotland's most famous soldiers. Lord Lovat was chief of Clan Fraser and commander of his own regiment, the Lovat Scouts. Lovat and his men were often in the front line against the Nazis. Achnacarry House, the home of Clan Cameron, was the secret base for training these special troops. It was renamed Castle Commando.

The men who trained here became the best soldiers in the British army. Some joined the Special Operations Executive or SOE. The SOE headquarters was at Arisaig on the far west coast of Scotland. Resistance fighters from all over Europe came here to learn the dirty tricks of war. Then they were dropped back into Europe by parachute to cause trouble for the Nazis. Many were caught and killed as spies, but their dangerous work did much to help defeat Hitler's Germany.

# Scots under Fire!

Thousands of Scots men and women served in the armed forces. Many joined the Royal Navy and the RAF and fought alongside men from all over Britain and the British Empire. Most Scots, however, joined the traditional Scottish regiments which were part of the army.

**Winston Churchill inspecting Scots troops at a victory parade in Germany, 1945.**

Scottish regiments were in the British army which was sent to France at the start of the war in 1939. The 51st Highland Division fought bravely in northern France in the summer of 1940. Greatly outnumbered, it was forced to surrender to the Germans at St Valery on the French coast. The Gordon Highlanders were in the British army which was defeated at Singapore by the Japanese in 1942. These were low points

Convoys were often targeted by German bombs. In this picture, taken in the North Atlantic in 1941, a bomb has narrowly missed hitting one of the convoy ships.

in the war for the British. They were worrying times for families back in Scotland with loved ones killed in action, taken prisoner or 'missing presumed dead'.

After 1942, the Allies were on the attack. The 51st Highland Division played its part in the great victory at El Alamein in North Africa. Scottish regiments were involved in the invasions of Italy and France and the final defeat of Germany in 1945. Scottish troops also fought in India and Burma helping to defeat the Japanese.

Many Scots fought in the war at sea. A number served in the North Atlantic convoys that brought much needed weapons and food from America. Others sailed up into the Arctic Ocean to deliver war supplies to the Russians. The

convoys and their naval escorts gathered and sheltered in the deep waters of Loch Broom and Scapa Flow before setting off on their dangerous missions. Many British convoy ships were sunk by German U–Boat torpedoes. Their shipwrecked crews often froze to death in the icy northern waters.

Even Scottish fishermen played a part in the war. Fishing boats from the northern ports secretly carried weapons across the North Sea from the Shetland Islands to Norway to help the resistance fighters there in their struggle against the Nazis.
This important link in the war effort became known as the 'Shetland Bus'.

# Letting off Steam

The war lasted for six long years. This was longer than anyone had imagined when it started in 1939. It was a worrying time, with shortages and air raids at home, and bitter fighting overseas. People needed to relax and 'let off steam'.

Most people had little money during the war, so pleasures had to be simple ones, and holidays had to be cheap. The government did not want people travelling around the country without a

good reason. The trains were needed for moving troops and valuable supplies such as coal. So the government encouraged 'Stay-at-Home' holidays. Councils organized cheap entertainments at holiday times such as open-air dances, sporting competitions and bonny baby contests. For many families, having a picnic in the country and a day away from the worries of the war, was a great treat.

In the towns and cities, many people went to the cinema almost every week. War films always showed the Allies winning in the end. One film, *Night*

Women dancing during a 1944 Stay-at-Home holiday in Aberdeen.

A huge wartime crowd watching a football match at Hampden Park, Glasgow.

*Train to Munich,* was very popular because it showed the Germans being outwitted by British heroes. Every night, most Scots tuned their radio wireless sets to the BBC. They listened to news of the war and to quiz and comedy shows. Dancing was also popular with many younger Scots. Every town had a hall where a local band played for the weekend dancers. The biggest ballrooms in Glasgow, such as the Locarno, could hold up to 2,000 people. By 1943, new American dances, such as the jitterbug, were all the rage.

Most sports stopped at the start of the war. The government thought that large football crowds would be an easy target for German bombers or for gas attacks. So the Scottish League and Cup competitions were suspended. Club players were called up into the armed forces. Later, the government realized that the troops wanted to see football, so special matches were held between regiments or between teams from the different armed services. One famous match was held at Hampden Park in 1944. Scotland played England and won by five goals to four.

# Women at War

By 1941, most Scottish men under forty years old had been called up to join the armed forces. This left fewer men to work in the factories making weapons, or on the farms growing food. Women took their places instead, doing important jobs in the war effort.

Right: Women at the Rolls Royce factory in Glasgow, made parts for fighter planes.

Below: Women were needed for skilled jobs making weapons in factories.

Many Scots women worked in munitions factories, making guns, shells and other military supplies. At Hillington, near Glasgow, Rolls Royce had an important aircraft factory which employed and trained a large number of 'craftswomen'. By 1943, almost half of

WOMEN OF BRITAIN
COME INTO
THE FACTORIES

the workers in Scotland's factories were women. Women also played a big part in the ARP. They served as fire-fighters, ambulance drivers and signal operators.

In the first years of the war, there was a great shortage of the wood needed to make aircraft and ships. Many Scottish women joined the Women's Timber Corps and helped to cut and process Scotland's forests. These women were often from towns and cities, but they quickly got used to country life.

In country areas, there was a shortage of workers on farms. Many women were directed into the Women's Land Army to help with the harvest.

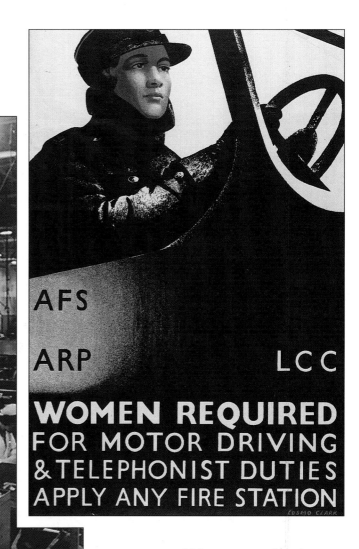

Women took jobs driving in the services so men could take on front-line duties.

After 1941, women were called up to serve in the armed forces. Many younger women joined the Auxiliary Territorial Service (ATS). These women did the jobs in the army that had to be done in Britain, so that soldiers could be sent to fight abroad. The Women's Auxiliary Air Force (WAAF) did important jobs in government offices, air-control towers and radar stations.

By 1941, women in uniform were an everyday sight in Scotland.

Ceaselessly new vehicles roll off the production lines. Army units await them, the ATS deliver them

Women from the Land Army parade down a street in Aberdeen, 1941. The Land Army helped to feed the British people by working on farms in the country.

Many women had homes and families to look after, so they could not join the services. They could only give up their spare time to help the country. They joined the Women's Voluntary Service (WVS). They did the dozens of everyday jobs that someone had to do, such as giving out food and clothing parcels to homeless, bombed-out families, or helping those who had lost relatives in air raids to cope with their loss. At every main railway station, there was a WVS canteen where servicemen could buy a cheap cup of tea and something to eat.

# Prisoners of War

On the night of 10 May 1941, a lone German Messerschmitt fighter plane was spotted by RAF radar crossing southern Scotland. Around ten in the evening, the plane crashed in a field near Eaglesham, but the pilot had already escaped using his parachute. Troops from the local Home Guard quickly found the burning wreck and the pilot, who happily gave himself up. They did not believe him when he said he was Rudolf Hess, Hitler's closest friend and deputy leader of the German Nazi Party.

Hess had flown secretly to Scotland to try and meet the Duke of Hamilton, a member of the Royal family. Hess had met the Duke at the 1936 Olympic Games in Berlin. He believed that Hamilton could influence the British Government and get a peace deal between Britain and Germany. Hess was only 19 km from the Duke's home when his plane crashed. After interrogation, he spent the rest of the war as the most famous prisoner captured in Scotland.

POWs were usually sent to live and work in small country villages.

German prisoners mending roads in 1942.

Many thousands of ordinary Germans, and their allies, the Italians, spent their war years as prisoners of war, or POWs, in Scotland. Usually, they were housed in rough camps and were set to do hard work such as repairing roads. In country areas, such as Angus, Perthshire and the Borders, POWs were sent to farms. There they were given food and shelter but they had to help with the farmwork.

Some prisoners were beaten up, usually by people who had lost friends and relatives in the war and who wanted revenge on the enemy. Most POWs, however, were treated well and were amazed by the kind treatment they got from the Scots. Very few German prisoners tried to escape from their camps and none managed to get out of the country.

POW Camp 60 was in the Orkney Islands. Several hundred Italian prisoners were housed here. They had been captured in North Africa and were far from home, lonely and bored. The British officer in charge of their camp gave them two Nissen huts to work in. Using scrap metal and pieces of old plasterboard, the Italian POWs turned them into a beautiful chapel which survives today. After the war, many Italian and some German POWs stayed on in Scotland, settled here and became Scots themselves.

The interior of the Italian Chapel was covered with plasterboard and finely decorated by an Italian prisoner of war called Domenico Chiochetti.

The Italian Chapel, Orkney.

# Victory

By the beginning of 1945, it was clear that Nazi Germany would soon be defeated. Allied troops were deep into German territory. On 30 April 1945, Hitler killed himself and on 7 May, the Germans surrendered. The war in Europe ended the very next day on 8 May 1945. The government made it a national holiday called Victory in Europe Day, or VE Day.

All over Scotland, families celebrated. Many people went to church for services of thanksgiving. Many went to public houses, but whisky and beer were in short supply in Scotland at that time. There were some street parties but very few Scots families could afford to buy Scottish flags or Union Jacks to hang out. These cost nine shillings (£1.08) from the department stores, and that was too much after six long years of war in which wages had been kept low.

Many Scottish families did not join in the celebrations. They had loved ones in the armed forces in the Far East. They were fighting the Japanese who had not yet been defeated. These men were expecting to fight more bloody battles in

Anti-tank obstacles, no longer needed, being broken up at Aberdeen Beach, April, 1946.

Churchill and his government waving to crowds in London on VE Day, 1945.

the jungles of Southeast Asia before invading Japan itself. Then, in early August, they heard news which meant they could go home. The Americans had dropped a new weapon, the atomic bomb, on the Japanese cities of Hiroshima and Nagasaki. The Japanese surrendered on 14 August 1945. World War II was over.

Within weeks, thousands of Scots servicemen were returning home from all over the world. Many arrived at a special centre at Leith Docks near Edinburgh where they were 'demobilized'. This meant they were no longer in the armed forces. Their uniforms and weapons were collected up, and they were issued with a set of everyday clothes. Some had been away from home for more than four years. Now they were civilians again. They could go back home and celebrate victory.

But thousands of Scots never returned home. They are buried in Commonwealth War Graves around the world and remembered on war memorials in every Scottish village, town and city.

Oor Wullie celebrating victory with the rest of his gang.

# Glossary

**Allies** The countries fighting Nazi Germany and Japan, centred on Britain, Russia and the USA.

**Ammunition** Bullets, shells and bombs.

**Armed forces** The army, navy and air-force.

**Atomic bomb** A very powerful bomb invented by the Allies to end the war quickly.

**Axis** The name given to the group of countries fighting the Allies. The Axis were Germany, Italy and Japan.

**Barracks** A group of buildings that house people in the armed forces.

**Battalions** Groups of 600–800 men in an army regiment.

**Blackout** A law forcing people to cover their lights at night.

**Blitz** A sudden air raid.

**British Empire** Britain and all the countries she rules over.

**Clan** A Scottish word for family.

**Cockpit** Where the pilot sits in a fighter plane.

**Convoys** Groups of ships carrying goods, accompanied by warships

**Corrugated** Sheet steel bent into a rippled shape to strengthen it.

**Evacuate** Remove people (evacuees) from a place of danger.

**Fritters** Pieces of food, usually potatoes, sliced and fried in batter.

**Front line** Position of army where there is contact and fighting with the enemy.

**Greens** Vegetables.

**Home Front** The war effort in Britain.

**Hot pot** A stew made from scraps of food.

**Interrogation** Questioning of prisoners.

**Lard** Fat from the stomach of a pig. It is used for cooking.

**Luftwaffe** The German air force.

**Master Race** German race Hitler believed was made to rule over all other peoples.

**Nazi** A member of the German National Socialist Party that was led by Hitler.

**Newsreel** A short film informing people of recent events that have happened.

**Nissen huts** Military shelters made from corrugated steel bent round in a semi-circular shape.

**Phoney** Something that isn't real.

**Rations** Fixed shares of food, petrol and clothing in short supply.

**Recruits** People who have just been employed to work in the armed forces.

**Recycle** Use again

**Regiments** Organized groups of people in the armed forces.

**Resistance fighters** Men and women in countries occupied by Germany who kept fighting the Nazis.

**Shrapnel** Pieces of hot metal scattered when a bomb explodes.

**Tanks** Armoured vehicles that carry heavy guns with tracks instead of wheels.

**Tenements** Buildings of several storeys with many people living in them. Built mainly in the cities of Scotland.

**Tenement closes** Public corridors or alleyways between tenement buildings.

**Trenches** Lines of ditches dug by soldiers to cover themselves from gun-fire.

**U-boats** German submarines.

**Wireless** An old-fashioned word for radio.

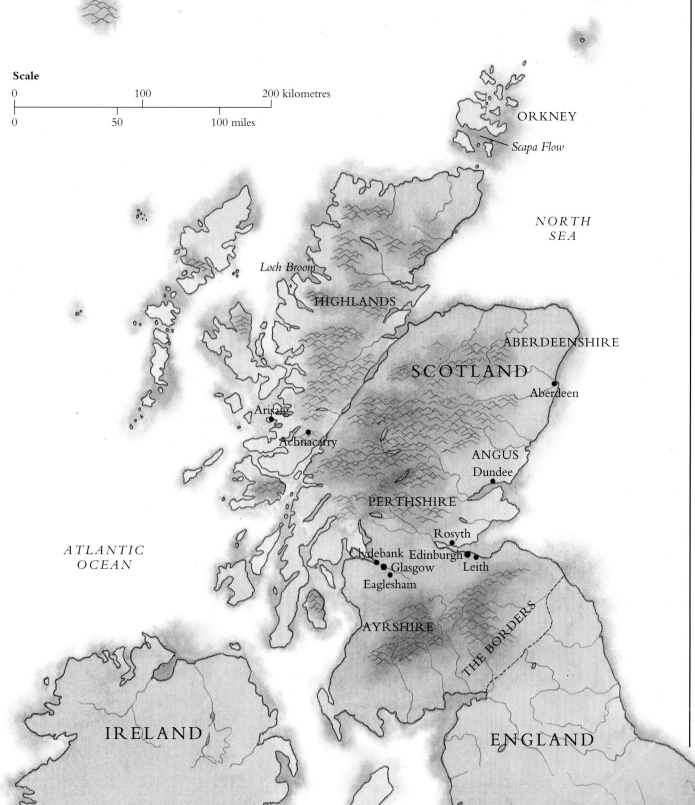

# Map of Scotland

### including places mentioned in the text

SHETLAND

**Scale**

0        100       200 kilometres

0     50      100 miles

ORKNEY

*Scapa Flow*

*NORTH SEA*

*Loch Broom*

HIGHLANDS

ABERDEENSHIRE

SCOTLAND

Aberdeen

Arisaig

Achnacarry

ANGUS

Dundee

PERTHSHIRE

Rosyth

Clydebank   Edinburgh

Glasgow     Leith

Eaglesham

*ATLANTIC OCEAN*

AYRSHIRE

THE BORDERS

IRELAND

ENGLAND

# Further Information

You can find out more about Scotland during World War II quite easily. Older people in your family, like your grandparents, may remember the war or know someone who does. Your school may have a logbook which tells what happened to the pupils between 1939 and 1945. Your community will have a war memorial that remembers the dead from your part of Scotland. You may find clues about the war in the local church or kirk yard. There are books and videos about the war that you can order from your local library.

Collections of aircraft from World War II can be seen at the Museum of Flight at East Fortune in East Lothian. Myreton Motor Museum at Aberlady houses a collection of British military vehicles from the war. Scalloway Museum in the Shetland Islands tells the story of the secret links between the Northern Isles and the Norwegian Resistance movement. Culzean Castle in Ayrshire contains wartime relics that show the links between the castle and the Allied Commander in Chief, General Eisenhower. The Scottish National War Memorial at Edinburgh Castle is a very impressive monument to the fallen Scots of both world wars. The Commandos are remembered at their memorial at Spean Bridge in the Highlands.

The regimental museums in Scotland all have sections relating to World War II. These include the Royal Scots Museum and the Scottish United Services Museum at Edinburgh Castle; the Argyll and Sutherland Highlanders Museum at Stirling Castle; the Gordon Highlanders Museum in Aberdeen; the Queens Own Highlanders Museum at Inverness; the Black Watch Museum in Perth; the Royal Highland Fusiliers Museum in Glasgow and the Cameronians Museum in Hamilton.

## Books to Read

*Oor Wullie Goes to War* (D. C. Thomson Publications, 1989).

*The Blitz, Evacuation, Prisoners of War, Propaganda, Rationing* and *Women's War* are all books in The Home Front series (Wayland, 1990).

## For reference:

W. Doran & R. Dargie, *Conflict & Cooperation 1930–1960* (Canongate Press, 1992).

I. Nimmo, *Scotland at War* (Archive and Scotsman Publications, 1989).

B. Osborne & R. Craig, *Scotland 1939* (Scottish Library Association, 1989).

*Aberdeen at War* (Archive and Aberdeen Journals Publications, 1987).

*'Far wis ye fin the Sireen blew?'* (City of Aberdeen Publications, 1993).

# Index